Discover & Learn

North & South America

This Activity Book is full of questions to help KS2 pupils improve their locational knowledge of North and South America.

Please note:
Pupils will need the matching CGP 'North & South America' Study Book to answer the questions in this Activity Book.

Published by CGP

Consultant: Joanna Copley

Authors: Catherine Hitchcock and Amanda MacNaughton

Editors: Mary Falkner, Sarah Pattison, Rebecca Russell, Caroline Thomson

ISBN: 978 1 78294 983 1

With thanks to Felicity Booth and Glenn Rogers for the proofreading.

With thanks to Jan Greenway for the copyright research.

Printed by Zenith Print & Packaging Ltd, Pontypridd.

Clipart from Corel®

Text, design, layout and original illustrations © Coordination Group Publications Ltd. (CGP) 2019

All rights reserved.

Photocopying this book is not permitted, even if you have a CLA licence.
Extra copies are available from CGP with next day delivery • 0800 1712 712 • www.cgpbooks.co.uk

Contents

Section One — The Continents

North America 2

South America 4

Natural Americas 6

Moving to the Americas 8

Section Two — Northern America

Greenland & Alaska 10

Northern and Western Canada 12

Eastern Canada 14

USA — East Coast 16

USA — In the Middle 18

USA — Out West 20

Section Three — Southern North America

Mexico and Central America 22

The Caribbean 24

Section Four — South America

Andean Nations 26

Brazil and the Guianas 28

The Southern Cone 30

The Southern Islands 32

Section Five — The Americas on the Globe

World Zones 1 34

World Zones 2 36

Section One – The Continents

North America

Read pages 2 and 3 of the Study Book about the countries of North America, then answer these questions.

1. Name the <u>countries</u> that are labelled A – D on the map below.

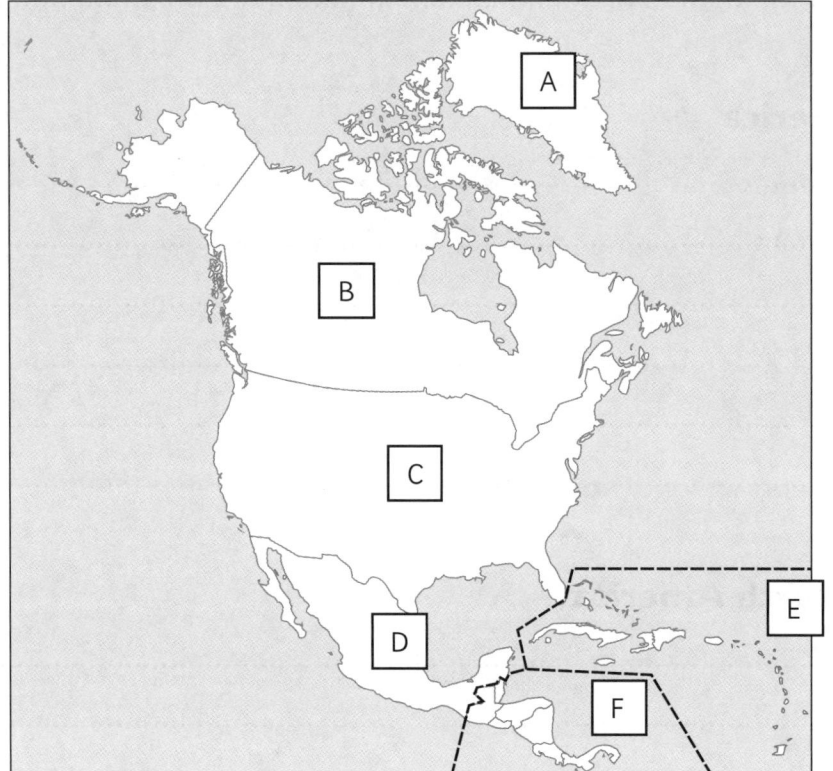

A = ...

B = ...

C = ...

D = ...

Name the <u>areas</u> that are labelled E and F on the map.

E = ...

....

F = ...

....

2. Read these postcards from North American places. Write which <u>country</u> each postcard has come from.

| The apartment I'm staying in is at the bottom of the Rocky Mountains. There are lots of trees and animals around, and I can see the Missouri River from my window. | I'm on a fishing holiday in the north of North America. It's quite cold and it looks like it might snow soon — but that won't stop me wrapping up warm and going fishing on the Mackenzie River. | I'm on a beautiful beach watching the sun set over the Pacific Ocean. The country I'm in is south of the USA. Tomorrow we're going hiking in the Sierra Madre mountains. |

....

3. Fill in the missing labels on this map of North America.

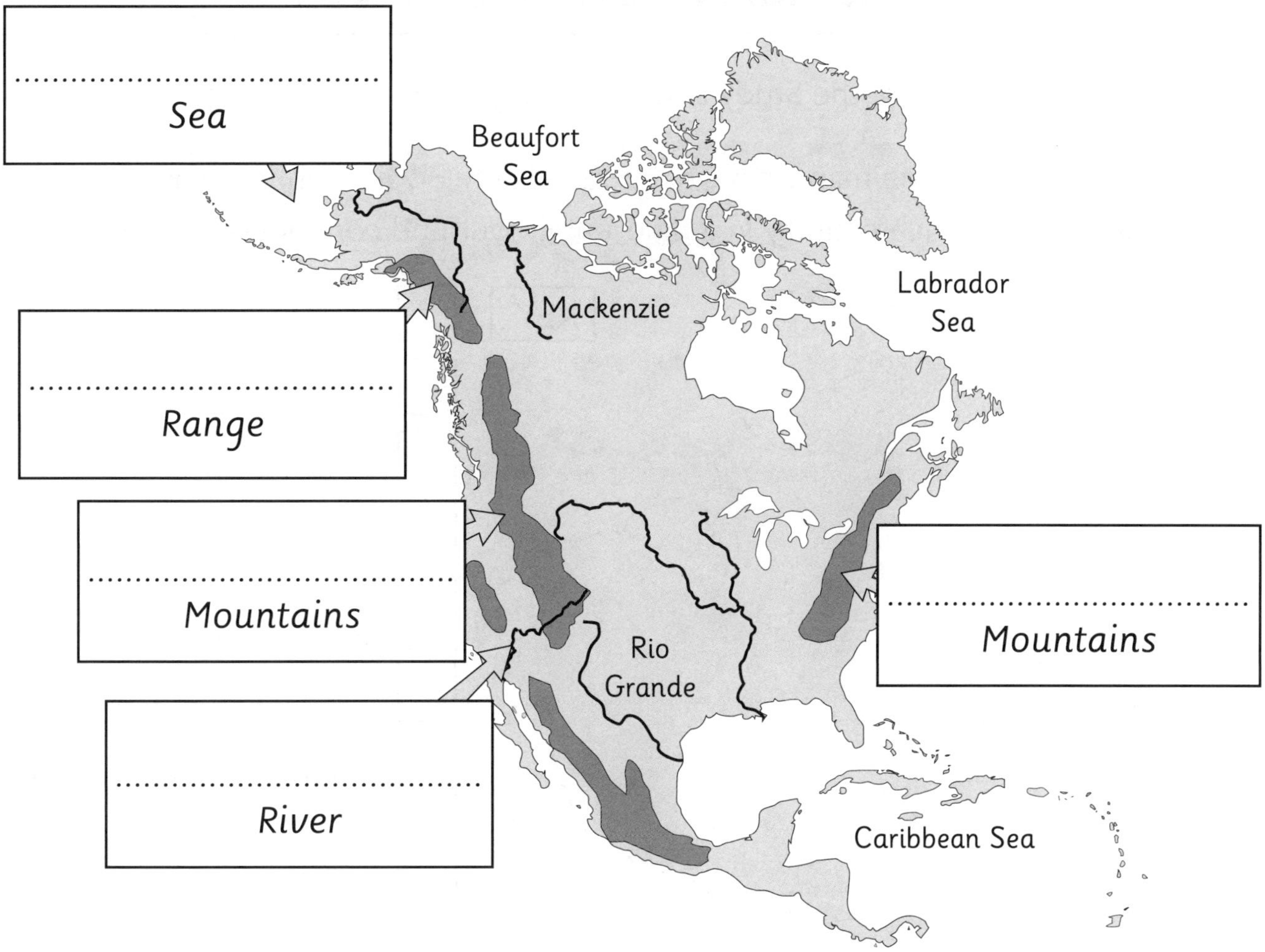

.... Sea

.... Range

.... Mountains

.... River

Beaufort Sea

Mackenzie

Labrador Sea

Rio Grande

.... Mountains

Caribbean Sea

4. Draw a line to match each fact to the correct country.

The largest island in the world.	USA
The smallest country in North America.	Saint Kitts and Nevis
The country with the longest shoreline in the world.	Greenland
A country that's split into 50 states.	Canada

"I can name and locate the main countries in North America and describe its physical geography."

South America

Look at pages 4 and 5 of the Study Book to help you answer these questions.

1. Look closely at the map on page 4 of the Study Book. On the map below, shade each country in a different colour and complete the key.

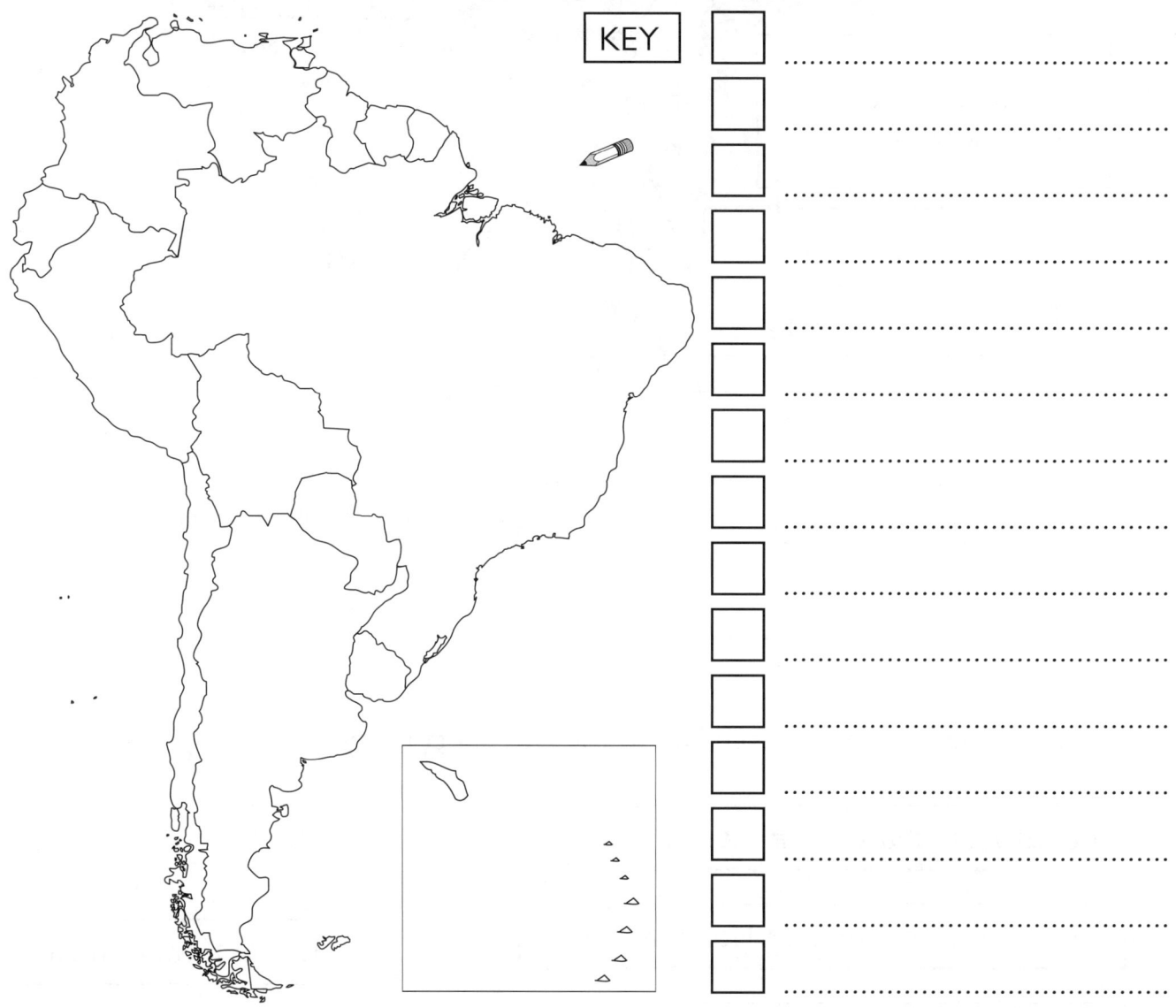

2. Colour in the names of the countries below that don't have any coastline.

Bolivia   Peru   Guyana   Colombia

Uruguay   Brazil   Paraguay

© CGP — not to be photocopied

3. Look at the maps on pages 4 and 5 of the Study Book.
   List the seven countries that the Andes mountains run through.

   1) ....   5) ....

   2) ....   6) ....

   3) ....   7) ....

   4) ....

4. Read each statement below and decide if it is true or false.
   Tick the correct box. Be prepared to explain your answer.

   The Amazon River is the longest in the world. True ☐ False ☐

   The Falkland Islands are located off the west coast of Chile. True ☐ False ☐

   The Paraná River travels through Brazil, Paraguay and Argentina. True ☐ False ☐

   About 7 million penguins live on the island of South Georgia. True ☐ False ☐

5. Choose one country in South America you'd most like to visit and give a reason why you chose this place.

   I would go to ....

   This is because ....

   ....

   ....

"I can name and locate the main countries in South America and describe its physical geography."

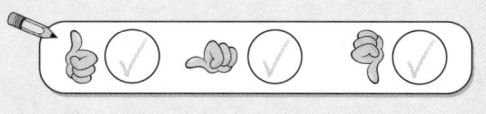

Natural Americas

Read pages 6 and 7 of the Study Book. Then answer these questions about the plants, animals and climates of the Americas.

1. Draw lines to match each country's label to its largest biome.

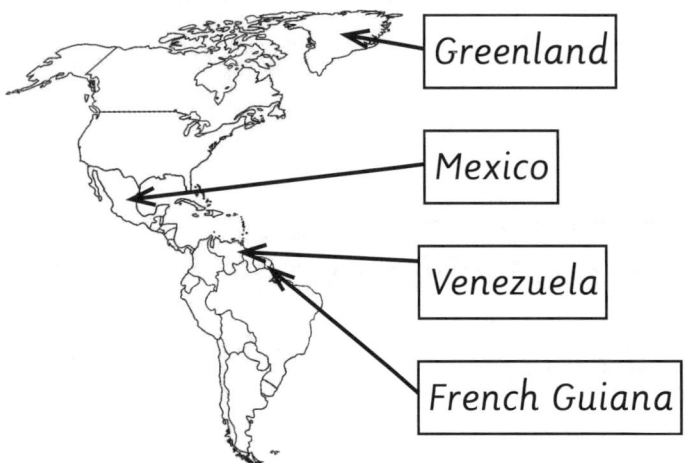

Greenland	Savannah
Mexico	Tropical Rainforest
Venezuela	Polar Desert
French Guiana	Desert

2. Read the information about the three animals found in the Americas. Which biome do you think they are each adapted to?

Fringe-toed lizard
- Light brown colour
- Can close flaps over its nose to stop sand getting in.

Red crossbill
- Large, overlapping beak which it uses to get seeds out of pine cones.

Chinchilla
- Thick, grey fur
- Its blood can carry lots of oxygen so it can live on very high ground.

Biome: ....

Biome: ....

Biome: ....

3. The pictures below show four different places in the Americas. Write the name of the biome that each picture shows.

1) ....

2) ....

3) ....

4) ....

4. Some scientists have predicted that there could be a 5 °C increase in global temperatures by the end of the century. If this happens, which biome do you think will be most under threat? Explain your answer.

I think the ....

biome will be most under threat, because ....

....

....

"I know about the different biomes in the Americas and some of the plants and animals found there."

Moving to the Americas

Look at pages 8 and 9 of the Study Book to help you answer these questions.

1. Read the clues and complete this crossword.

Across

3 Some of the Powhatan tribe lived in these round houses.

5 This killed a lot of indigenous people.

6 This language is commonly spoken in Central and South America.

7 This is the official language of Quebec in Canada.

Down

1 The original people of a particular place are called the _____ people.

2 This is the name of an Inca city in Peru.

4 These people mostly worked on sugar plantations.

2. Write down one advantage of having a 'melting pot' of different cultures in the USA.

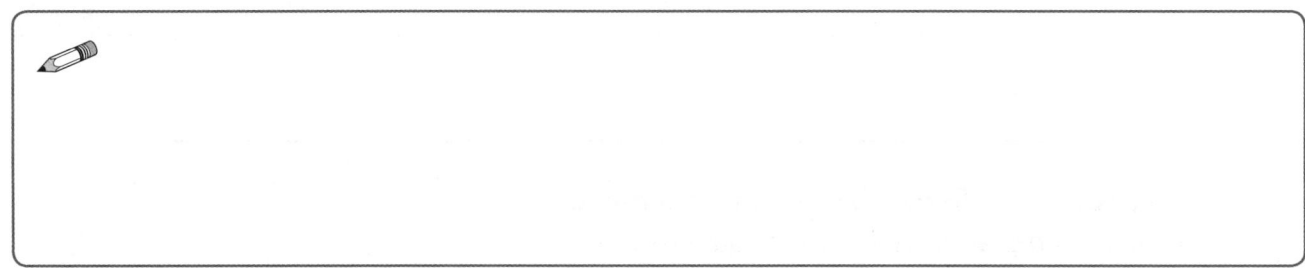

3. European settlers completely changed the Americas. Write down two negative effects of European settlers moving to the Americas and setting up colonies.

1) ....
   ....

2) ....
   ....

4. Use the information on pages 8 and 9 of the Study Book to solve the clues and fill in the words below. Then unscramble the letters in the grey boxes to make a word that the Americas have lots of.

Christopher Columbus claimed the Caribbean for this country.
☐ _P_ _ _ _N

A type of food brought to the Americas from Poland.
_ _ _G_ ☐ _

One of the countries that set up colonies in the Americas in the 1600s.
_ _ ☐ H ☐ _ L _ _ _ _ _

A word that means forcing people to work.
_ L _ _ _ _ ☐ Y

One of the countries that used to be home to the Inca empire.
E ☐ ☐ _ D _ _

The name of a tribe of indigenous people in Canada.
_ _ ☐ _ T

The scrambled up word is ....

"I know some of the reasons why people moved to the Americas and the effects it has had on the culture."

Section Two – Northern America
Greenland & Alaska

Read pages 10 and 11 of the Study Book, then answer these questions.

1. Read each sentence and circle <u>Greenland</u> or <u>Alaska</u> to show whether the <u>fact</u> relates to Greenland or Alaska.

   It's one of the 50 states of the USA. — Greenland / Alaska

   It's almost completely covered by glaciers. — Greenland / Alaska

   Its most important industry is oil and gas. — Greenland / Alaska

   The capital city is Juneau. — Greenland / Alaska

   The most important industry is fishing. — Greenland / Alaska

2. Some of the Inuit people in Greenland still have very <u>traditional</u> lifestyles. Others have more <u>modern</u> lifestyles. Read what the Inuit man says below about his <u>traditional</u> way of life. Using the information on page 11 of the Study Book, fill in the <u>speech bubble</u> for the boy, describing what you think his <u>less traditional</u> daily life might be like.

Inuit tradition is very important to me. This morning I got up very early to go hunting. I might be out here for several days with my dogs. It's very cold, but I need to hunt to get food and warm clothes for my community.

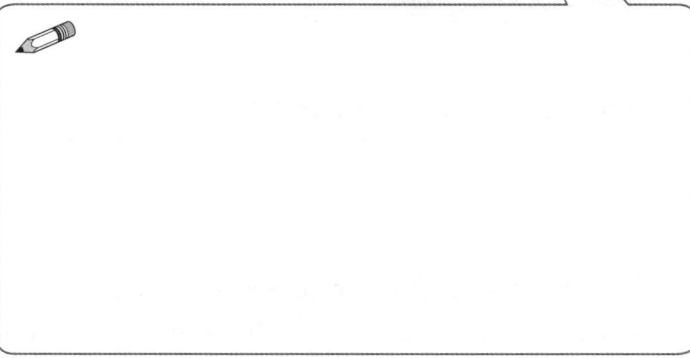

© CGP — not to be photocopied

3. Why do people in Greenland mostly live around the coast? Give two reasons.

1) ....
   ....

2) ....
   ....

4. Look at the statements below. Colour any statements that are most likely to apply to an Inuit living 50 years ago in blue. Colour any statements that are most likely to apply to an Inuit today in red.

| I work in an office. | I fish from sea ice. | I travel by sled. |

| I travel by snowmobile. | I hunt for everything I need. |

5. Look at the map on page 10 of the Study Book. On the map below, draw a dotted line to show the position of the Arctic Circle.

"I can locate Greenland and Alaska on a map and I know about their geography and the people who live there."

Northern and Western Canada

Look at pages 12 and 13 of the Study Book to help you answer these questions.

1. Look at the map on page 12 of the Study Book. Draw a line to match each city to the province or territory of Canada that it's in.

Edmonton	British Columbia
Vancouver	Alberta
Regina	Nunavut
Winnipeg	Manitoba
Iqaluit	Saskatchewan

2. Look at the information on page 13 of the Study Book. Use it to help you complete the fact files below for Nunavut and Saskatchewan.

You can also look at the biomes map on pages 6 and 7 of the Study Book.

	Nunavut	Saskatchewan
Biome(s)		
Products mined there		
Major industries		

© CGP — not to be photocopied

3. The photograph shows a house built on <u>stilts</u>, which is common in Nunavut. <u>Why</u> are many houses in Nunavut built like this?

Houses in Nunavut are built like this

because ....

....

....

....

....

4. The graph below shows the average monthly temperatures in <u>Whitehorse</u> in Yukon. Look closely at the graph and <u>complete</u> the sentences below.

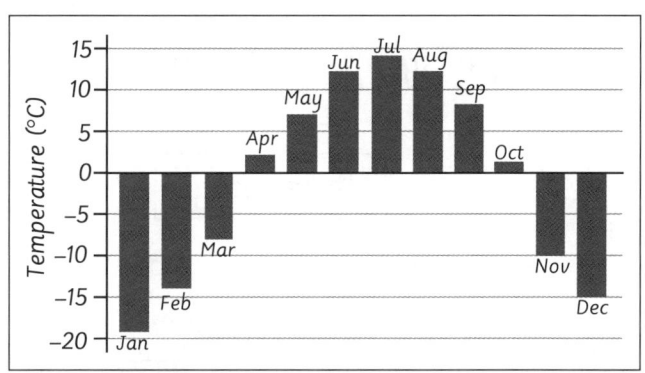

The coldest month in Whitehorse is ....

The average temperature in this month is ....

The warmest month in Whitehorse is ....

The average temperature in this month is ....

The first month of the year where the average

temperature is above 0 °C is ....

"I can name and describe the provinces and territories of northern and western Canada."

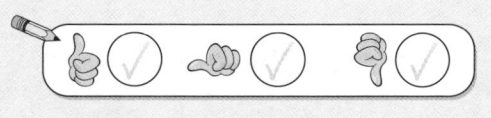

Eastern Canada

Pages 14 and 15 of the Study Book tell you about the six provinces that make up eastern Canada, and some of the things they're known for.

1. Unscramble the letters in the grey boxes to find the answers to the clues.

   A river in Ontario — banlay

   Halifax is in this province — anov saoict

   An animal found in Quebec — fowl

   The ocean to the east of Canada — talcinta

   A province famous for maple syrup — cebequ

   One of the Great Lakes — lkae hnruo

2. Use the words in the box below to fill in the passage about the Great Lakes.

   | Lake Erie | UK | five | Lake Superior | USA | Lake Ontario |

   The Great Lakes make up part of the border between Canada and the .... There are .... Great Lakes in total. .... is the furthest west and .... is the furthest east. The Niagara River flows from .... to Lake Ontario. All together, the area of the Great Lakes is almost the same as the area of the ....

3. Look at the information about <u>hydroelectricity</u> on page 15 of the Study Book. Read the statements below, then <u>label</u> the diagram with the numbers 1, 2 and 3 to show <u>where</u> each of the <u>three stages</u> takes place.

| 1) Water is diverted from rivers into underground tunnels. | 2) The tunnels take the water to the turbines. | 3) The water turns the turbines to generate electricity. |

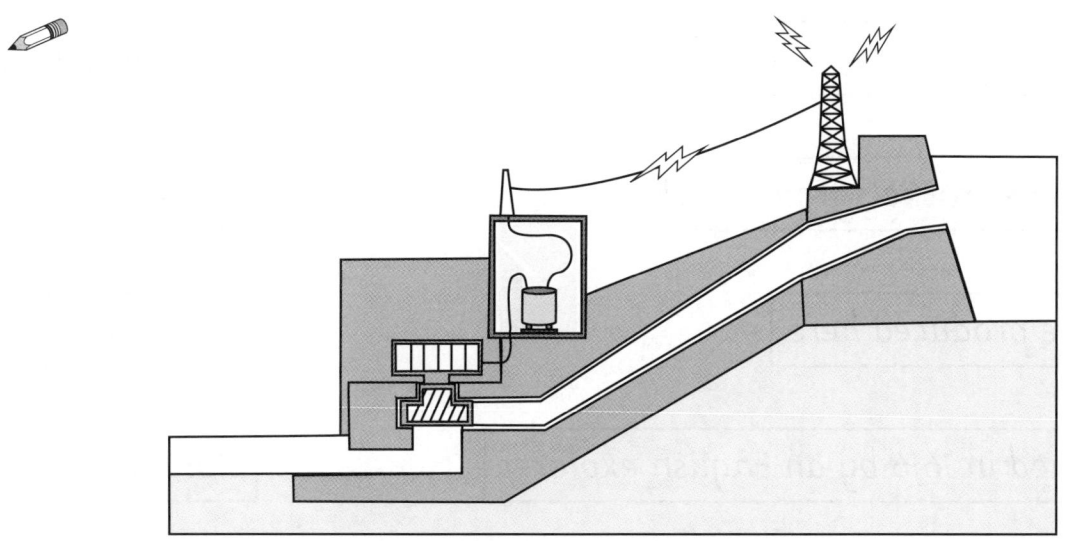

4. Imagine that you're a <u>tourist</u> visiting Niagara Falls. Write a postcard to a friend to <u>describe</u> what you have seen and done. Don't forget to draw a <u>stamp</u>.

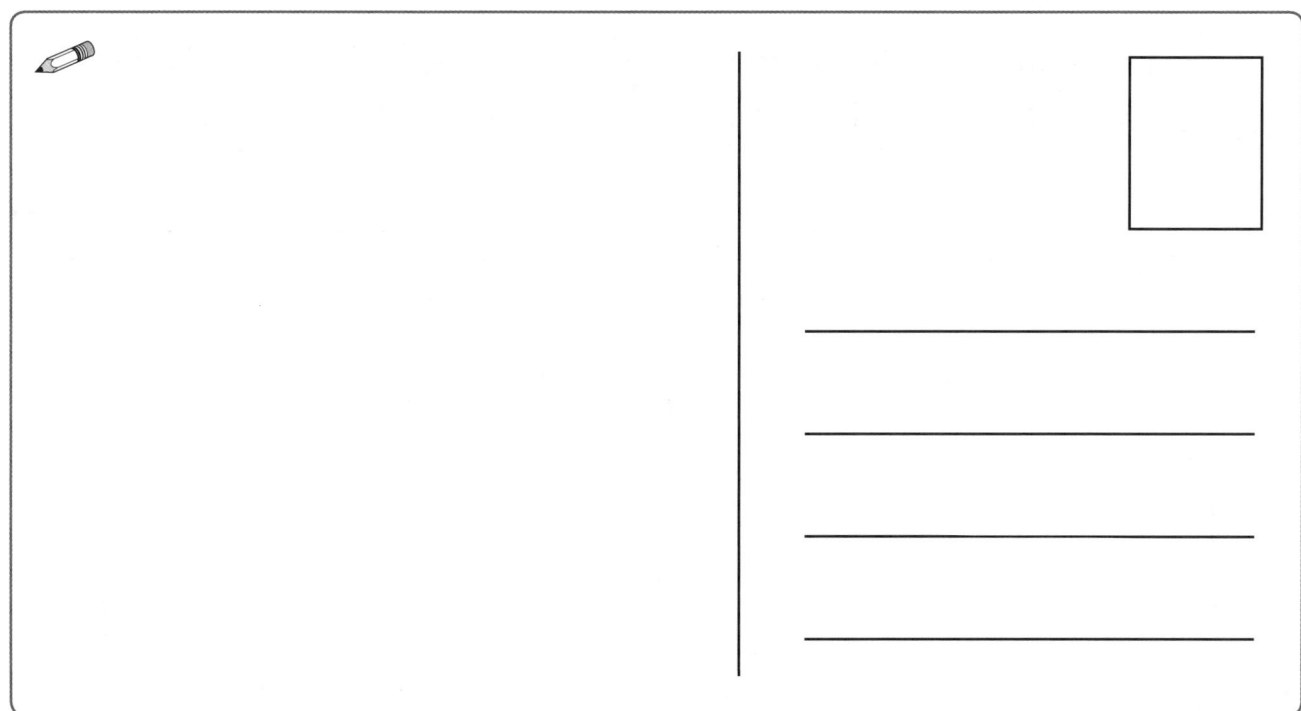

"I know about the provinces of eastern Canada and their geography."

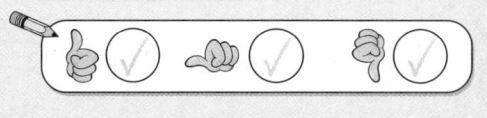

USA – East Coast

Read pages 16 and 17 of the Study Book to help you answer these questions.

1. Look at the map on page 16 of the Study Book. Draw a line to match each of these facts to the correct location.

The President of the USA lives here.	Washington D.C.
NASA launches rockets from here.	Georgia
Peanuts are produced here.	Cape Canaveral
It was named in 1616 by an English explorer.	Florida
Walt Disney World® is located here.	New England

2. Imagine you have visited both Vermont and southern Florida in <u>winter</u>. <u>Draw</u> what you might have seen from your <u>window</u> in each place.

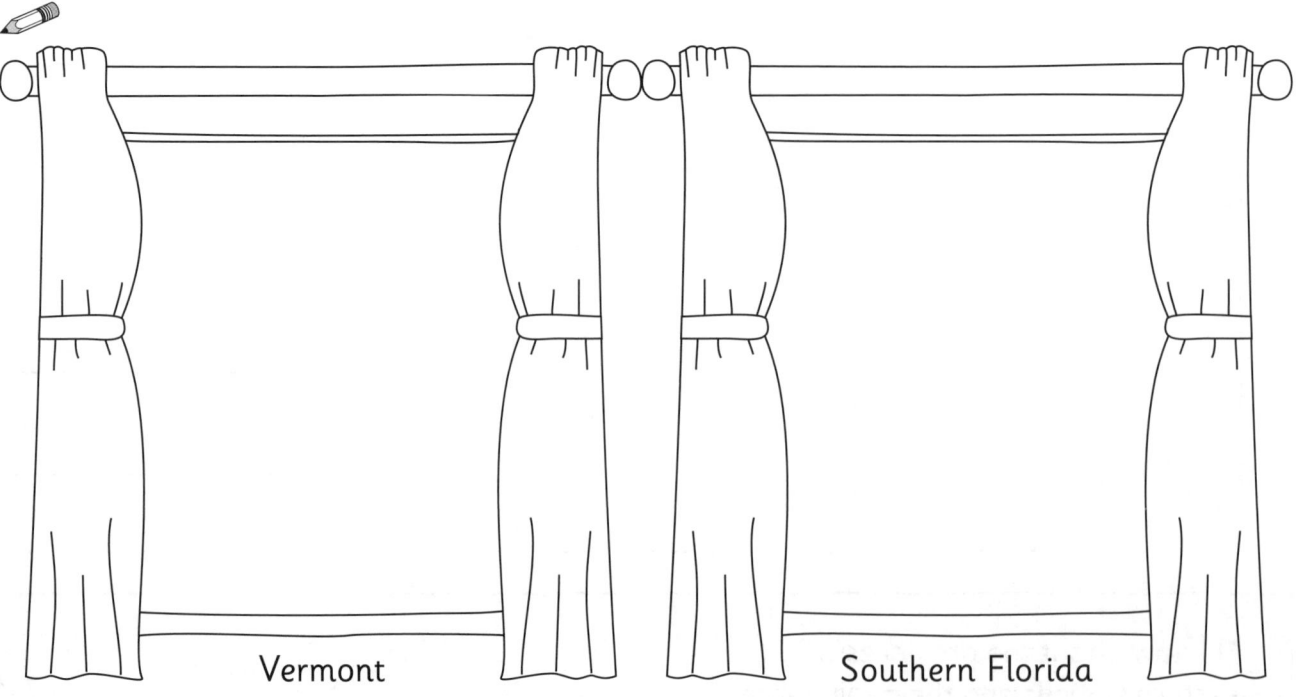

Vermont   Southern Florida

© CGP — not to be photocopied

3. The <u>economy</u> is how a country or region <u>makes</u> and <u>uses money</u>. Why do you think Walt Disney World® in Florida is important for the local <u>economy</u> of the East Coast of the USA?

I think Walt Disney World® is important for the local economy because

....

....

....

4. Some scientists think the <u>temperatures</u> on the East Coast of the USA could <u>rise</u> by up to 4 °C by the end of this century. What <u>problems</u> do you think this temperature change might cause for <u>tourists</u> in Vermont and Florida?

Vermont:	Florida:

5. Would you prefer to visit <u>Vermont</u> or <u>southern Florida</u> as a tourist? <u>Explain</u> your answer.

I would prefer to visit .... *because*

....

....

....

"I know the states that make up the East Coast of the USA and some of the things they're famous for."

USA – In the Middle

Read pages 18 and 19 of the Study Book to help you answer these questions.

1. Look at the map on page 18 of the Study Book. Write the names of the places or things being described in the boxes.

Many homes in 'Tornado Alley' have one of these.

This rocky feature took 14 years to carve.

This river flows through North and South Dakota.

The Mississippi River begins in this state.

2. Read the newspaper article below about some of the good and bad sides of oil production. Do you think Texas should continue to produce oil? Give a reason for your answer.

Texas oil — good or bad?

The oil industry is a very important part of the economy in Texas and in the USA. But it has downsides. Producing and burning oil creates greenhouse gases and other chemicals that can be harmful to the environment. Sometimes, oil gets spilled and can end up poisoning drinking water. Drilling for oil can even cause earthquakes in the area. However, local resident Lara Khan supports the oil fields. "Drilling for oil gives jobs to hundreds of thousands of people in Texas," she said. "Texas exports oil all around the world to people who need it, and it earns us billions of dollars."

I think / don't think Texas should continue to produce oil, because

....

....

....

....

....

....

3. The Mount Rushmore sculpture is a giant sculpture of the four presidents of the USA that the <u>artist</u> thought were the most <u>important</u>. Who is important to you that you would include in a giant sculpture? <u>Draw</u> them below and <u>label</u> your drawing to say <u>who</u> they are and <u>why</u> you chose them.

4. What would happen to <u>rice production</u> in Louisiana if there was a decrease in <u>rainfall</u> and <u>less water</u> in the Mississippi River? What effect would this change have on the <u>local economy</u>?

Decreased rainfall and water in the Mississippi would mean ....

....

This would affect the local economy because ....

....

....

"I know the states that make up the middle of the USA and some of the things they're famous for."

USA – Out West

Pages 20 and 21 of the Study Book are about the western states of the USA.

1. Complete these statements correctly and write them into the grid. What is the phrase running down the centre of the grid?

   1. The south-western states have large sandy ....
   2. California is located next to a .... plate boundary.
   3. The .... River begins in Colorado.
   4. Yellowstone National Park is in the state of ....
   5. San Francisco and Los Angeles are both cities in ....
   6. Mount St Helens is a .... in Washington.
   7. The .... Fault runs through California.
   8. The hottest air temperature on Earth was recorded in ....
   9. The 1980 eruption of Mount St Helens created a huge .... cloud.
   10. .... is a famous city in the state of Nevada.
   11. .... is a city in the state of Hawaii.
   12. Google is a big .... company near San Francisco.
   13. The .... is a famous steep-sided valley in Arizona.

The phrase is

....
....

2. Read the information in the speech bubbles below and decide which state each person is from.

> I live in a state that has a border with Canada and Idaho.
> My sister said she saw a bear when she was rafting on the Missouri River yesterday.

> I live in a state that borders Mexico. It's really hot and the southern part of the state is a desert. Some people are convinced a UFO landed here once, but I don't think it's true.

This person is from

....

This person is from

....

3. The Grand Canyon is a popular tourist attraction. Can you think of two damaging things that might happen when lots of tourists visit a place?

Think about what tourists might bring or do, and what they might leave behind.

1) ....

2) ....

4. In your own words, explain what a geyser is and why it erupts.

A geyser is ....

....

It erupts because ....

....

....

"I know the states that make up the western USA and some of the things they're famous for."

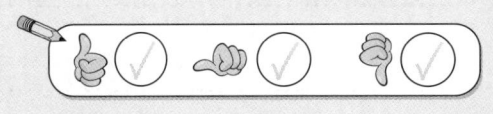

Section Three – Southern North America
Mexico and Central America

Look at pages 22 and 23 of the Study Book to help you answer these questions.

1. <u>Complete</u> the map of Central America by <u>labelling</u> the countries listed below.

   Costa Rica   Panama   El Salvador   Guatemala
   Belize   Honduras   Nicaragua   Mexico

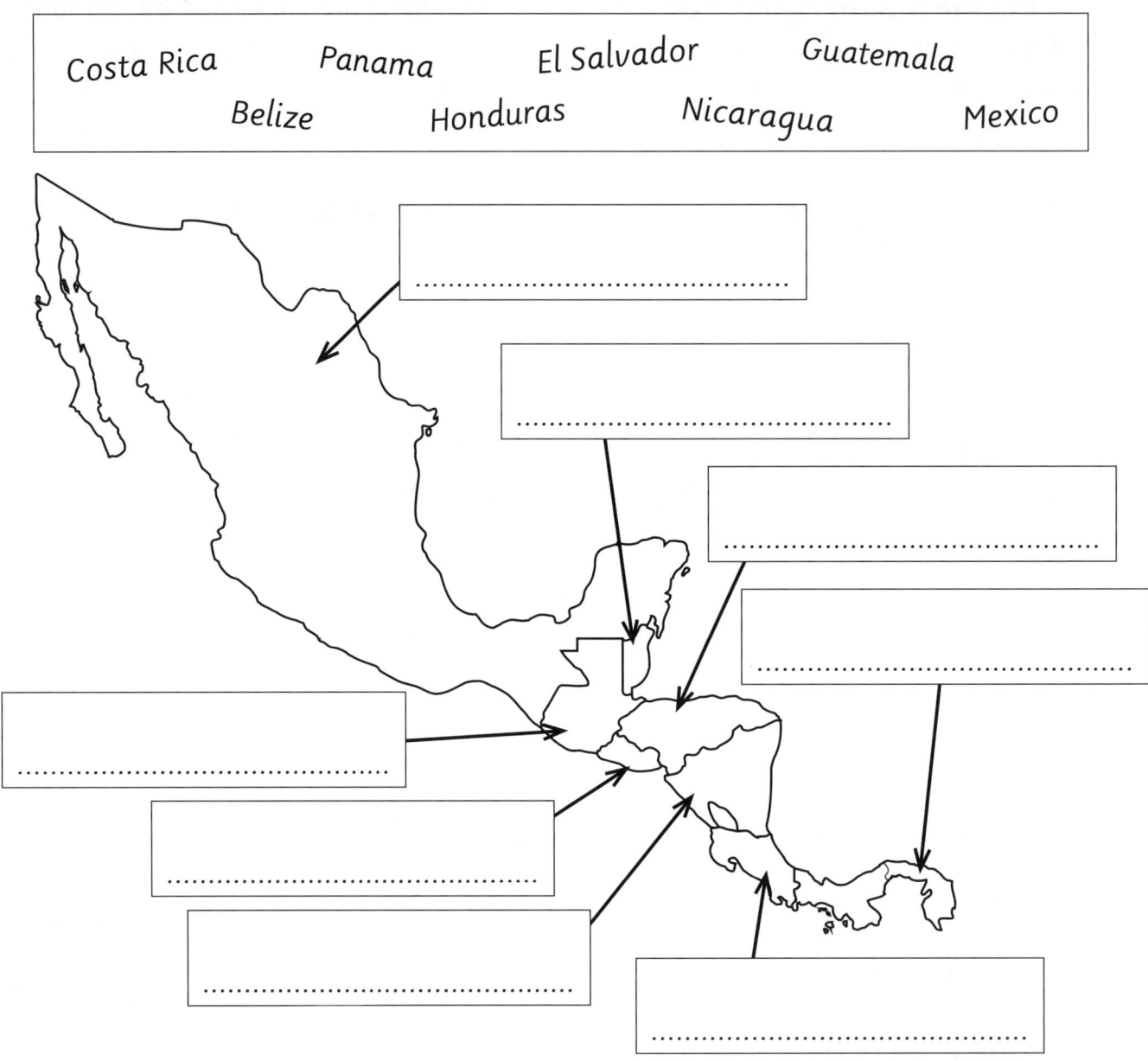

2. Why is Central America a good place to grow <u>bananas</u>?

   ....
   ....
   ....

© CGP — not to be photocopied

3. Look at the pictures of living things found in the Chihuahuan Desert. Draw lines to match the statements below to the correct pictures.

| large fleshy stem to store water |

| large eyes to help to spot predators |

| white underbelly deflects heat from the ground |

| long, narrow tail to help to turn when running |

| sharp spines to protect from animals that try to eat it |

| long toes to help to run up to 20 miles per hour |

4. Decide if each statement below is true or false, and tick the correct box.

There were already people living in Central America when the Spanish colonised the area in the 1500s.   True ☐   False ☐

Many volcanic eruptions occur in Central America because the countries sit on the Ring of Fire.   True ☐   False ☐

The wide range of temperatures in Mexico means that only a few types of plants and animals can survive there.   True ☐   False ☐

The Chihuahuan Desert covers an area of Mexico and Guatemala.   True ☐   False ☐

"I can name and locate the countries of Mexico and Central America, and describe the biomes found there."

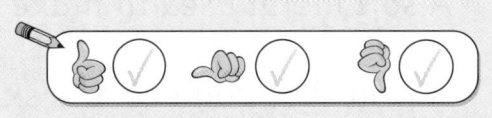

The Caribbean

Pages 24 and 25 of the Study Book are about the Caribbean Islands.

1. Read the information about flags below, and then <u>design a flag</u> that could represent the <u>union</u> of the countries of the <u>Caribbean</u>.

   Flags are used to represent groups of countries, as well as separate countries. The choice of colours and shapes on flags can symbolise different things. For example, stars can be used to represent different states or countries in a region, and stripes of colour could represent the land and the sea. Some countries' flags have pictures of the plants or animals found there.

   Think about colours and symbols that could represent the Caribbean region.

2. Use the clues below and the information on page 24 of the Study Book to <u>fill in</u> the missing letters from the words. Each word is an <u>export</u> from the Caribbean.

Clue						
Used to sweeten food and drink.		u			r	
A fruit with sharp leaves on its top.			n	a		
This bean is used to make chocolate.	c			o		
A soft metal used to make jewellery.			l		r	
A fruit that you peel the skin from.		a		a		a

© CGP — not to be photocopied

3. Find the names of the Caribbean Islands listed below in this word search. There's one island hidden in the grid that isn't in the list — can you find it?

Anguilla
Antigua
Aruba
Bahamas
Barbados
Cayman Islands
Cuba
Dominica
Grenada
Guadeloupe
Haiti
Jamaica
Martinique
Puerto Rico
St Kitts and Nevis
St Lucia
St Vincent

B	V	A	B	Q	S	E	O	N	A	R	S	I	C	O	R	S	I	H
P	O	I	V	C	T	V	T	A	G	A	T	G	R	E	N	A	D	A
T	R	M	F	A	V	X	P	J	V	J	K	A	N	T	I	R	K	T
Z	A	O	R	Y	I	S	P	L	J	A	I	T	G	A	B	U	W	S
F	S	N	I	M	N	J	U	T	A	M	T	S	C	J	A	T	G	G
A	R	T	C	A	C	O	E	R	S	A	T	I	R	A	H	A	M	U
N	Q	S	Z	N	E	B	R	O	L	I	S	U	V	H	A	I	A	A
G	U	E	T	I	N	E	T	M	I	C	A	X	S	A	M	T	R	D
U	D	R	S	S	T	A	O	J	K	A	N	J	H	B	A	O	T	E
I	G	R	E	L	F	H	R	V	A	U	D	E	T	A	S	U	I	L
L	A	A	U	A	M	R	I	T	O	A	N	C	O	R	A	Q	N	O
L	J	T	V	N	F	G	C	W	Y	L	E	M	S	B	O	V	I	U
A	P	N	P	D	H	A	O	R	R	S	V	U	B	A	S	V	Q	P
A	J	Y	X	S	A	R	H	B	S	T	I	M	U	D	I	G	U	E
B	D	A	N	T	I	G	U	A	C	L	S	R	A	O	B	J	E	A
I	T	L	A	S	T	P	I	T	T	U	K	L	I	S	X	N	D	O
A	M	D	O	M	I	N	I	C	A	C	A	M	T	C	U	B	A	P
P	E	N	N	Q	B	A	R	H	U	I	J	O	P	P	R	M	F	Q
G	U	A	C	T	A	I	G	U	V	A	R	U	B	A	A	O	R	S

The hidden island is ....

4. Who brought calypso music to the Caribbean and what was it used for?

....
....
....
....

"I know about the different islands of the Caribbean, and their culture and history."

Section Four – South America

Andean Nations

Read pages 26 and 27 of the Study Book about the countries that the Andes mountains run through, then answer these questions.

1. Write two statements about the Andean nations using the words 'highest' and 'tallest'.

   1) ....
   ....

   2) ....
   ....

2. Draw lines to match each name below with the right fact.

Name	Fact
Lake Titicaca	is the second largest producer of copper and silver in the world.
Peru	is in Venezuela.
The Andes	is the capital city of Colombia.
Lake Maracaibo	is caused by humidity and heat.
Angel Falls	are 7200 km long.
Catatumbo lightning	is the second biggest of its kind in South America.
Bogotá	is 979 metres high.

© CGP — not to be photocopied

3. Read page 27 of the Study Book, then complete the speech bubbles to show how different life is in the mountains and in the city.

Where I live is

Where I live is

4. Read the statements below about mining. Decide whether they are good points or bad points. Colour the good points in green, and the bad in red.

Mines are used to get tin, copper, iron and other useful metals.

Mining can release toxic chemicals into the environment.

Sometimes rocks fall and gases explode in mines.

Homes may be destroyed to make space for mines.

Mining provides fuel which can be used for heating and transport.

Mining helps people in poor areas to earn money.

"I can name and locate the northern Andean countries and describe some of their interesting features."

Brazil and the Guianas

Read pages 28 and 29 of the Study Book, then answer these questions.

1. Complete this crossword.

Across
1 This country was once ruled by the Netherlands.
4 French Guiana is still a part of here.
5 The Yanomami and Guarani are two _____ .
7 Brazil has these to help protect the rights of the tribes.
8 Cutting down large areas of trees.

Down
2 Tropical parts of South America contain dense wooded areas known as _____ .
3 The Pantanal is the world's largest _____ .
6 The largest South American country.

2. Tropical rainforest covers a large part of Brazil and the Guianas. Name three human activities that endanger the rainforest.

1) ....

2) ....

3) ....

3. The Yanomami people depend of the forest to live. The survival of their culture depends on continuing to live in these traditional ways. Imagine you're a member of the Yanomami tribe and you're trying to persuade the miners not to cut down the forest where you live. What would you say? Use page 29 of the Study Book to help you write a short speech.

4. Read the facts below about deforestation in the rainforest to find out why it happens. Do you think deforestation should be stopped? Why or why not?

Rainforest and Deforestation Facts:
- Every minute, an area of forest the size of 20 football fields is cut down.
- Rainforests are home to about half of the plant and animal species in the world.
- Trees are needed to harvest timber to make paper, furniture and houses.
- Land that is cleared by deforestation can be used for farming.
- The land that is cleared is only good for farming for a short time.
- The plants and trees of the rainforest produce oxygen, which we need to breathe.

I think deforestation should / shouldn't be stopped, because ....

....

....

....

"I can find Brazil and the Guianas on a map and I know about some of the issues affecting people there."

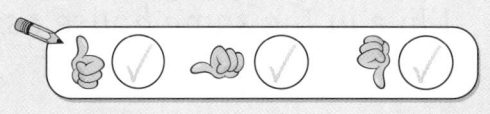

The Southern Cone

Read pages 30 and 31 of the Study Book, then answer these questions about the countries at the bottom of the South American continent.

1. Circle the countries and oceans that each country borders.

   Chile borders Paraguay / Argentina / Uruguay / Atlantic Ocean / Pacific Ocean

   Argentina borders Uruguay / Paraguay / Chile / Atlantic Ocean / Pacific Ocean

   Paraguay borders Chile / Argentina / Uruguay / Atlantic Ocean / Pacific Ocean

   Uruguay borders Argentina / Chile / Paraguay / Atlantic Ocean / Pacific Ocean

2. Which of the following words would not be used to describe the Atacama desert? Circle two words.

   dry   boiling   cool   large   hilly   flat

3. Look at the following statements from people living in Buenos Aires. Tick the correct box to show whether you think they are rich or poor.

	Rich	Poor
I own a financial business in the city.	☐	☐
When I grow up, I'll go to university.	☐	☐
I work in a factory in the city.	☐	☐
The apartment I live in is carefully guarded.	☐	☐
I live in the same house as many other people.	☐	☐

On the right is a picture of the Pampas in Argentina.

4. Draw lines to match each <u>word</u> to its <u>definition</u>.

| Pampas | | A large area of flat land. |

| Gauchos | | A large plain covering an area of South America. |

| Plain | | South American cowboys. |

4. Describe the <u>climate</u> of the Pampas.

Look at the map on pages 6 and 7 of the Study Book if you need help.

5. Using pages 30 and 31 of the Study Book for help, use the following <u>numbers</u> to write <u>four facts</u> about the Southern Cone.

| 9 million | 70,000 | 1960 | 1800 |

1) ....

2) ....

3) ....

4) ....

"I can name and locate the countries in the Southern Cone and describe some things they're known for."

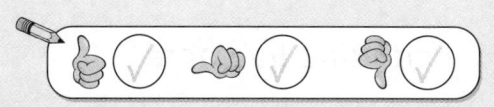

© CGP — not to be photocopied

The Southern Islands

Read pages 32 and 33 of the Study Book, then answer these questions about the islands at the bottom of South America.

1. Why don't many people live on the Southern Islands?

   Not many people live on the Southern Islands because ....

   ....

2. Look at the image of the Drake Passage on page 32 of the Study Book. Why do you think it's so dangerous to sail across?

   Hint: look at what's happening in the picture.

3. Read the statements and decide whether they are about the Falkland Islands (F), South Georgia and the South Sandwich Islands (S) or both. Tick the correct box for each statement.

Statement	F	S	Both
People only visit these islands or stay for a few months; no one actually lives here permanently.			
It's cold and windy here.			
About 3000 people live here.			
Fishing is the main industry here.			
Penguins live here.			

4. Label the features of this penguin using the words in the box.
   Explain why each part makes them well-adapted to a cold climate.

   waterproof feathers   blubber   strong claws

Waterproof feathers ....

Blubber ....

Strong claws ....

5. If you could visit either the Falkland Islands or South Georgia and the South Sandwich Islands, which one would you choose and why?

I would visit ....

because ....

....

....

"I can locate the Falkland Islands and South Georgia and the South Sandwich Islands and describe how the climate affects life there."

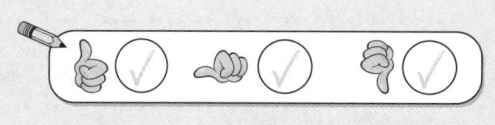

34 Section Five – The Americas on the Globe

World Zones 1

Read page 34 of the Study Book to see the imaginary lines that split up the Earth.

1. Explain in your own words what <u>latitude</u> means.

   ....

   ....

2. Use the information on page 34 of the Study Book to solve the <u>clues</u> below and fill in the <u>crossword</u>.

Across

6 The imaginary line around the middle of the Earth at 0° latitude.

7 The latitude of La Paz is this many degrees south.

8 Brazil is on this continent.

Down

1 The regions north of the Arctic Circle and south of the Antarctic Circle are called the _____ regions.

2 What latitude is measured in.

3 City at a latitude of 46° N.

4 The southern tip of South America at a latitude of 56° S.

5 The area between the Arctic Circle and the Tropic of Cancer is a _____ zone.

3. Look at the maps on page 34 of the Study Book. Would you expect <u>Montreal</u> to be <u>hotter</u> or <u>colder</u> than <u>La Paz</u>? Explain why.

   I would expect Montreal to be .... *than La Paz, because*

   ....

   ....

© CGP — not to be photocopied

4. Use the <u>map</u> below to answer each of the questions.

Which city is on the Equator?

....

What is the latitude of La Serena?

....

Which city is north of 20° N?

....

Do you think the climate of Quito will be more similar to the climate of Paramaribo or the climate of La Serena? Explain your answer.

I think the climate of Quito will be more similar to ....

because ....

....

5. Look at the maps on page 34 of the Study Book. Which of the three <u>climate zones</u> is each of the <u>cities</u> below found in?

Montreal: ....

Cape Horn: ....

Alert: ....

La Paz: ....

"I know about the Equator and other lines that split the planet up into climate zones."

World Zones 2

Read about the different climate zones on pages 34 and 35 of the Study Book.

1. Colour in the map below to show the different climate zones in Central and North America. Fill in the key to show which colour represents which zone. Label the three lines.

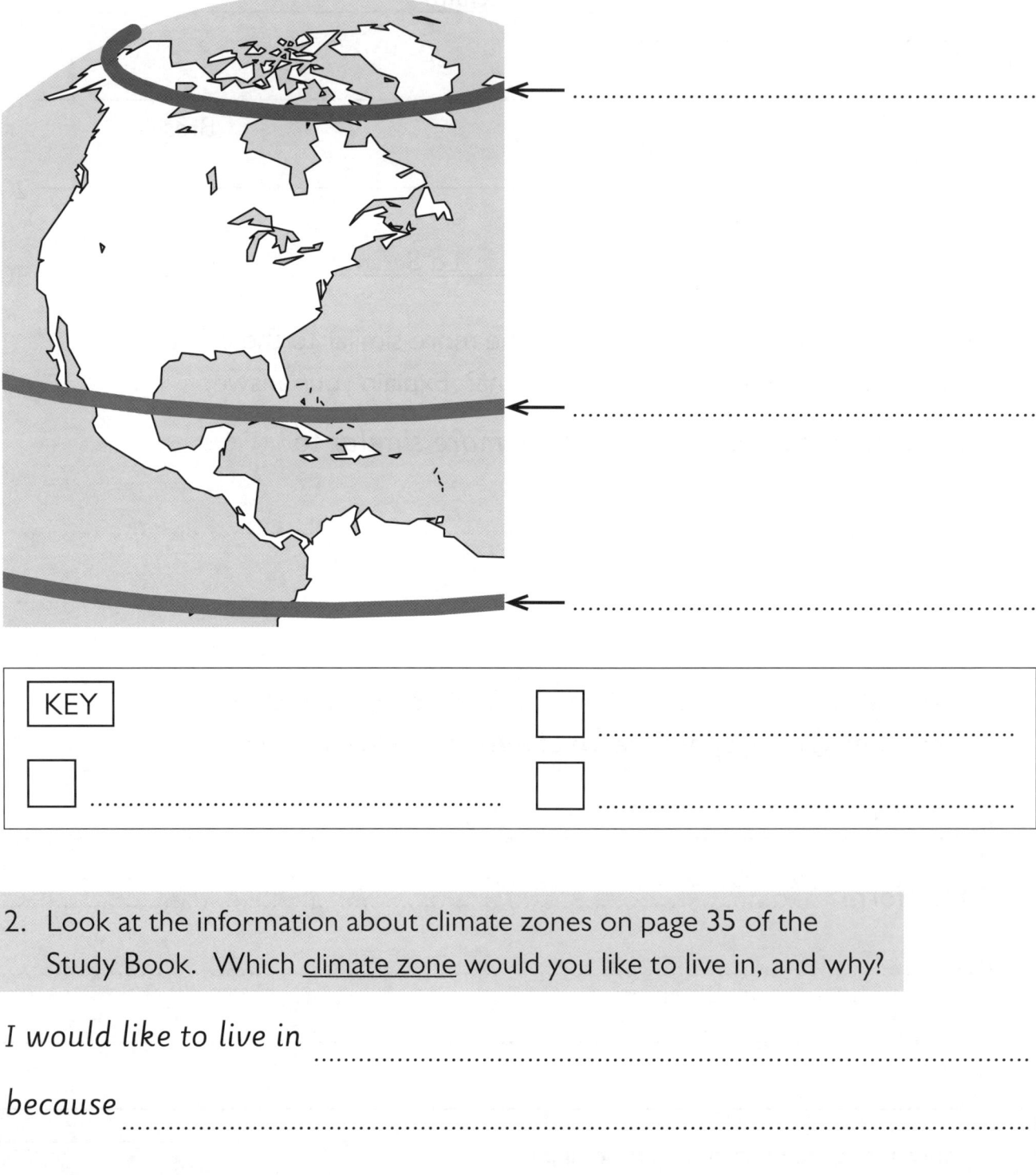

| KEY | ☐ .... |
| ☐ .... | ☐ .... |

2. Look at the information about climate zones on page 35 of the Study Book. Which climate zone would you like to live in, and why?

I would like to live in ....

because ....

....

3. Join the descriptions of the climates with the right climate zones.

The Tropics

The Polar Regions

The Temperate Zones

The summers are dry and winters are cold.

It is always hot.

There are four seasons.

It is always cold.

This climate zone is closest to the equator.

There are ice caps.

4. Imagine you're on a journey from the North Pole to the Equator. Draw a picture of what you might see in each climate zone.

Don't forget to label each drawing with the name of the climate zone.

"I know about the three main climate zones on the Earth and what their climates are like."

Acknowledgements

Cover photo © iStock.com/BardoczPeter

p6 (crossbill) © clarst5 / Shutterstock.com

p6 (lizard) © Clement Philippe / Arterra Picture Library / Alamy Stock Photo

p10 (inuit boy) © ton koene / Alamy Stock Photo

p10 (inuit man) © blickwinkel / Alamy Stock Photo

p13 (house on stilts) © Henk Meijer / Alamy Stock Photo

p27 (Andes) SL_Photography / iStock Editorial / Getty Images Plus

p27 (Lima) © Sean Sprague / Alamy Stock Photo

p29 (Yanomami) © Pulsar Imagens / Alamy Stock Photo

Thumb illustration used throughout the book © iStock.com